D1443888

Cows Can MOO! Can You?

Spring has sprung, my fine friends!
Come along! Grab an arm.
Let me take you to tour
the Greenbean family's farm!

The Cat in the Hat's Learning Library®
introduces beginning readers to basic non-
fiction. If your child can read these lines,
then he or she can begin to understand the
fascinating world in which we live.

Learn to read. Read to learn.

This book comes from the home of

THE CAT IN THE HAT

RANDOM HOUSE

For a list of books in **The Cat in the Hat's
Learning Library**, *see the back endpaper.*

The editors would like to thank
BARBARA KIEFER, Ph.D.,
Charlotte S. Huck Professor of Children's Literature,
The Ohio State University, and
MICHAEL VAN AMBURGH, Ph.D.,
Lindsay Chamberlain, Emily Chittenden, and other members of
Cornell University Dairy Science Club,
Cornell University, Department of Animal Science,
College of Agriculture and Life Sciences,
for their assistance in the preparation of this book.

Visit us on the Web!
Seussville.com
rhcbooks.com

Educators and librarians, for a variety of teaching tools, visit us at RHTeachersLibrarians.com

Library of Congress Cataloging-in-Publication Data
Names: Worth, Bonnie, author. | Ruiz, Aristides, illustrator. | Mathieu, Joe, illustrator.
Title: Cows can moo! Can you? : All about farms / by Bonnie Worth ;
illustrated by Aristides Ruiz and Joe Mathieu.
Other titles: All about farms | Cat in the Hat's learning library.
Description: First edition. | New York : Random House, 2018. | Series: The Cat in the Hat's lear
library | Includes index.
Identifiers: LCCN 2017016800 | ISBN 978-0-399-55524-4 (trade) | ISBN 978-0-399-55525-1 (lib.
Subjects: LCSH: Farms—Juvenile literature.
Classification: LCC S519 .W67 2018 | DDC 630—dc23

Printed in the United States of America   10 9 8 7 6 5 4 3 2 1

First Edition

Random House Children's Books supports the First Amendment and celebrates the right to read.

Cows Can MOO!
Can You?

by Bonnie Worth

illustrated by Aristides Ruiz and Joe Mathieu

The Cat in the Hat's Learning Library®

Random House 🏠 New York

Spring has sprung, my fine friends!

Come along! Grab an arm.

Let me take you to tour

the Greenbean family's farm!

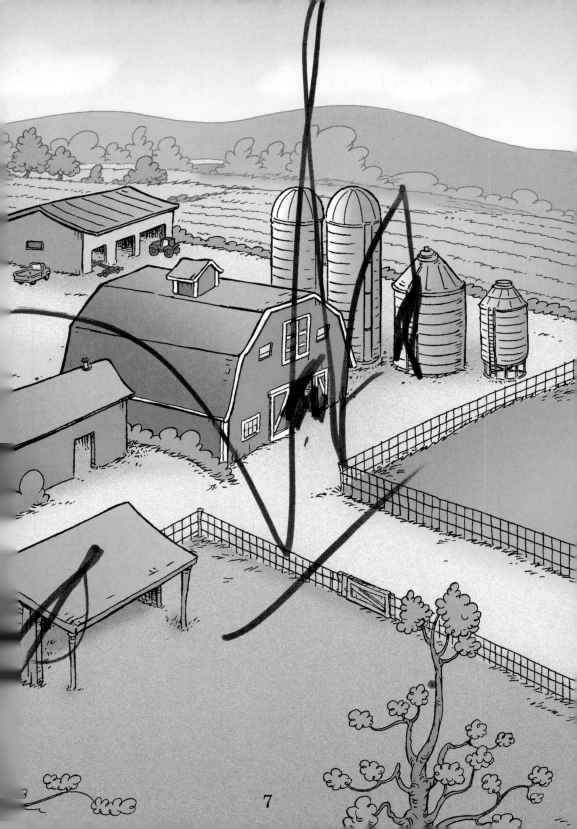

The sun's barely up—
and what do you know?
The house lights are on
with the rooster's first crow.

He stretches his neck
and says *cock-a-doodle-doo!*
Does that sound like the way
our day begins, too?

COCK-A-DOODLE-DOO!

9

The machines go *chuff-chuff*,
and the cows go *moo-moo*.
They clean udders beforehand
and when they are through.

Feeding the chickens
is not at all hard.
Just spread grains and seeds
all over their yard.

SCRITCH!

SCRITCH!

SCRITCH!

Pawk!

Pawk!

Nothing moves like a chicken
or talks like one talks.
Its claws go *scritch-scritch,*
and its beak *pawk-pawk-pawks!*

SCRITCH!

pawk!

k!

CATCHING

In the sheepfold, Mr. Greenbean
shears the sheep's belly fleece,
then he shaves off the rest
in one big neat piece.

Mr. Greenbean tries
to be gentle and quick,
to never pinch skin
or to hurt or to nick.

LAMB

SHEARING

Baaaa-baaaa!

Most sheep sound alike—
the lamb, ram, and ewe.
They all go *baaaa-baaaa!*
and have woolly fleece, too.

RELEASING

EWE

RAM

15

Mrs. Greenbean places
the wool on a table
and pulls out the tags—
as much as she's able.

SKIRTING

The tags are the wool
from the belly and back,
too dirty to use
so they're tossed in a sack.

tags

Next, she washes and dries it
and . . .

WASHING

. . cards out the knots.
his task takes some time
ause knots—there are lots!

Then she spins the wool
into a thick yarn—and that's
what she uses to knit
Greenbean mittens and hats.

SPINNING

In the truck garden's
tidy vegetable beds
are lettuce and kale
with tiny green heads.

Underground, carrots sprout.
They are actually roots.
Aboveground, the pole beans
put out their first shoots.

LETTUCE

CARROTS

Dean's hoe digs for weeds
and it *scratch-scratch-scratches*.
(The scarecrow is dressed in
an outfit that matches.)

E BEANS

TOMATOES

KALE

19

With tractor and tiller,
Mr. Greenbean needs
to ready the soil
for the planting of seeds.

TILLER

TRACTOR

Then Greenbean hitches up
the manure spreader
to fertilize the soil—
make it richer and better.

Suddenly, there comes
a loud, banging *crunch*!
A bent tractor axle
would be my best hunch.

But Mr. Greenbean,
being smarter than smart,
calls the tractor shop
to get a new part.

AXLE

With axle in place,
all shiny and new,
there is one more thing
Mr. Greenbean must do.

He'll hook up the planter
because, as he'll show,
it will spit out the seeds
in a nice, even row.

PLANTER

Spit Spit Spit

here goes the planter—
it-spit-spit-spit!
does the job quick
d is neat about it.

25

We leave and come back
on a dry summer's day,
when it's time for the Greenbeans
to bring in the hay.

SICKLE MOWER

The sickle mower cuts
down the field of tall hay.
Then it's left out to dry
for at least one more day.

The hay rake *swish-swishes*.

It goes to and fro

to gather the hay

into piles, like so.

WINDROWS

HAY RAKE

This long pile of hay—

all good farmers know—

is by a name.

It's called a windrow.

SWISH-SWISH

Here comes the baler
with a loud, rumbling roar,
packing hay into bales
that are easy to store.

RRRUUUUMMMBBLLLE!!!

BALER

BALE

28

Vroom-vroom goes the skid steer

as sister and brother

stack up the bales

one on top of the other.

29

Everything's green
and growing quite well,
till midsummer comes
and brings a dry spell.

This means the Greenbeans
must now irrigate.
They soak the dry soil
after dark, when it's late.

Like a big garden sprinkler,
the irrigator whips round
and waters the crops
with a *whap-whapping* sound.

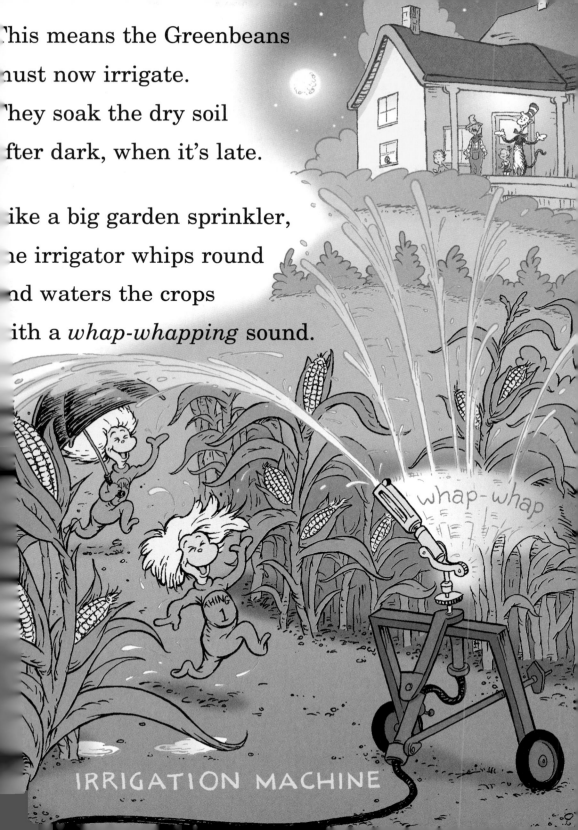

whap-whap

IRRIGATION MACHINE

Come fall, we return
for the harvest and reaping,
a date we have all
looked forward to keeping.

COMBINE

The combine does two
of the harvesting jobs.
It cuts down corn stalks
and cuts kernels off cobs.

32

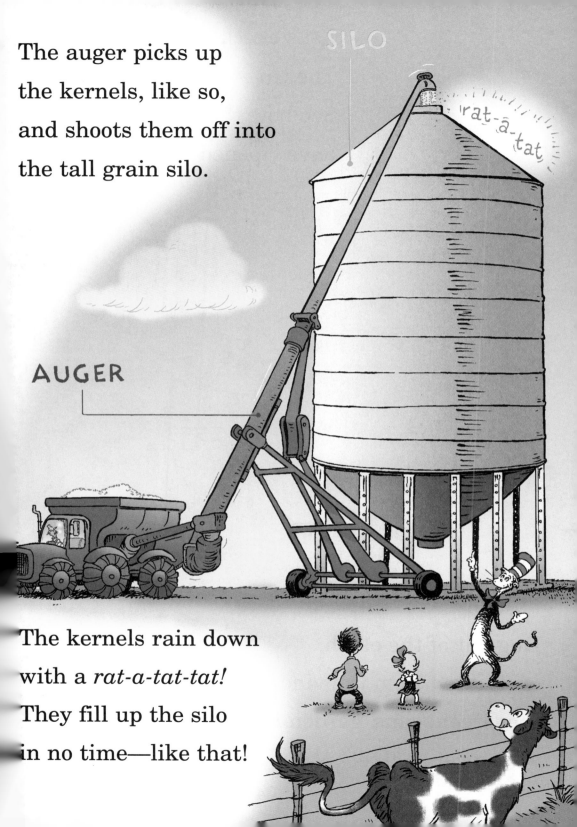

The auger picks up
the kernels, like so,
and shoots them off into
the tall grain silo.

SILO

rat-â-tat

AUGER

The kernels rain down
with a *rat-a-tat-tat!*
They fill up the silo
in no time—like that!

Let's check out the garden.
The time—how it's flown!
See how the veggies
have ripened and grown?

Dug out of the earth
or plucked from the vine,
the Greenbeans' garden harvest
was never so fine!

Let's load up the truck.
We must not delay,
or—didn't you know?—

heir noses *sniff-sniff*.
nells GREAT! What is that?
farm-fresh meal
om—

the Cat in the Hat!

GLOSSARY

Auger: A screw-shaped tool in a long metal tube used to move grain from the ground up to the top of a silo or grain bin.

Axle: A rod that passes through a wheel or group of wheels.

Dairy parlor: The part of a dairy barn where the cows are milked by machine.

Irrigate: To supply water to land or crops.

Kernel: The seed and hard cover from an ear of corn or a shaft of wheat.

Linger: To stay, perhaps longer than necessary, because you don't want something to end.

Manure: Animal dung used for enriching soil.

Sickle mower: A machine that cuts down tall grass or grain.

Spell: An unspecific period of time.

Truck garden: A field where vegetables are grown for market.

FOR FURTHER READING

A Kid's Guide to Keeping Chickens by Melissa Caughey (Storey Publishing). This excellent guide to raising chickens (winner of the AAAS/Subaru SB&F Prize for Excellence in Science Books) is perfect for families looking to start their own flock. For ages 8 and up.

Milk: From Cow to Carton by Aliki (HarperCollins, *Let's-Read-and-Find-Out Book*®). A guided tour of all the steps involved in making milk—from green grass to cow to the dairy to your refrigerator! (Also check out Aliki's *Corn Is Maize: The Gift of the Indians* in the same series.) For ages 4 to 8.

Total Tractor! (DK Children). Illustrated throughout with clear, detailed photographs, this overview of tractors—from vintage classics to modern machines—can be enjoyed by the whole family. For ages 7 to 10.

A Year at Maple Hill Farm and *Our Animal Friends at Maple Hill Farm* by Alice and Martin Provensen (Aladdin). Written and illustrated by a Caldecott Medal–winning husband-and-wife team, these two charming picture books about life on a New England farm are a delight. For ages 3 to 8.

INDEX

The Cat in the Hat's Learning Library

The Cat in the Hat's Learning Library

The Cat in the Hat's Learning Library

The Cat in the Hat's Learning Lib

The Cat in the Hat's Learning Library

The Cat in the Hat's Learning Library

The Cat in the Hat's Learning Li

The Cat in the Hat's Learning Library

The Cat in the Hat's Learning Library

The Cat in the Hat's Learning L

The Cat in the Hat's Learning Library

The Cat in the Hat's Learning Library

The Cat in the Hat's Learning

The Cat in the Hat's Learning Library

The Cat in the Hat's Learning

The Cat in the Hat's Learning Library®

Can You See a Chimpanzee?

Clam-I-Am!

Cows Can Moo! Can You?

Fine Feathered Friends

A Great Day for Pup

Hark! A Shark!

High? Low? Where Did It Go?

Hurray for Today!

I Can Name 50 Trees Today!

Ice Is Nice!

If I Ran the Dog Show

If I Ran the Horse Show

If I Ran the Rain Forest

Inside Your Outside!

Is a Camel a Mammal?

Miles and Miles of Reptiles

My, Oh My—a Butterfly!

Oh Say Can You Say DI-NO-SAUR?

Oh Say Can You Say What's the Weather Today?

Oh Say Can You Seed?

Oh, the Pets You Can Get!

Oh, the Things They Invented!

Oh, the Things You Can Do That Are Good for You!

On Beyond Bugs!

Once upon a Mastodon

One Cent, Two Cents, Old Cent, New Cent

One Vote, Two Votes, I Vote, You Vote

Out of Sight Till Tonight!

Safari, So Good!

There's a Map on My Lap!

There's No Place Like Space!

A Whale of a Tale!

What Cat Is That?

Who Hatches the Egg?

Why Oh Why Are Deserts Dry?

Wish for a Fish

Would You Rather Be a Pollywog?